Stress and Anxiety

*Practical ways to restore health
using complementary medicine*

Dr Adrian White

A GODSFIELD BOOK

Library of Congress Cataloging-in-Publication Data Available

10 9 8 7 6 5 4 3 2 1

Published in 1999 by Sterling Publishing Company, Inc.
387 Park Avenue South, New York, N.Y. 10016

DESIGNED FOR GODSFIELD PRESS BY
THE BRIDGEWATER BOOK COMPANY LTD

Picture research *Lynda Marshall*
Illustrations *Kevin Jones Associates* and *Michael Courtney*
Studio Photography *Zul Mukhida*

Distributed in Canada by Sterling Publishing
c/o Canadian Manda Group, One Atlantic Avenue, Suite 105
Toronto, Ontario, Canada M6K 3E7
Distributed in Australia by Capricorn Link (Australia) Pty Ltd
P O. Box 6651, Baulkham Hills, Business Centre, NSW 2153, Australia

Printed and bound in Hong Kong

ISBN 0-8069-3134-5

CONTENTS

INTRODUCTION

S TRESS IS A COMMON *feature of modern life, and for one in 20 people it is a severe problem. Stress involves fear, undermines our fundamental state of well-being, and makes us feel inadequate, because we tend to blame ourselves for suffering stress. However, nobody is born knowing how to handle pressure – everyone has to learn, one way or another.*

This book is written from a firm belief that if you understand what happens to you when you are under stress, you will be better able to cope. The changes that take place in your brain and your body when you are under stress are described in detail. Once you have understood these, you will realize how and why various approaches can help manage stress, and you will be able to choose the approaches that suit you best.

Stress is sometimes seen as an inevitable part of civilization, the price we have to pay for being insulated from physical dangers

LEFT *You will probably try various approaches to cope with stress.*

6

and not having to worry about
where our next meal comes
from. However,
the knowledge
and skills that
civilization offers
can also be applied to
effective stress management.

ABOVE *You may be
burning the candle
at both ends.*

The common causes of stress are problems
with the family, work, finance, or illness.
Whether you are someone who was always a
worrier, or someone who is stressed for the
first time, there is no doubt that you can be
helped to achieve your recovery. Sometimes
you may need professional help, and this
book tells you when and how to get the help
you need. Above all, remember that you are
not alone in your experiences: it can be a
great help knowing that others are recovering
from their stress. Your own stress, however, is
quite individual, and this book offers enough
choice so you can choose what is most relevant
and helpful for you.

WHAT IS STRESS?

The word "stress" is used in different ways. It can refer to the challenges of everyday life, which do not always cause us problems. But the word is also used for the feeling inside us if we cannot respond to the challenge. The medical term for this is anxiety.

ANXIETY

Everybody has experienced anxiety, and it serves a purpose. When you feel anxious before a performance of some kind, it "gets the adrenalin going" and brings out the best in you. For instance, anxiety felt before interviews or examinations means that the mind is as alert as possible. Sometimes, however, anxiety gets in the way: if you are too anxious before a driving test, for example, you might become so clumsy that it interferes with your performance. However, within a short time afterward, the anxiety settles down and you are back to normal.

TOO MUCH STRESS

A person can only take so much stress before he or she begins to feel uncomfortable. The mind and body become agitated: there is a vague sense of fear

BELOW *Work is piling up and you can't cope. This creates sleeplessness, which makes work even harder – it's a vicious circle.*

VICIOUS CIRCLES

There are two ways in which stress can become involved in a vicious circle, feeding upon itself and growing ever greater. First, you become mentally agitated and fatigued, and therefore less able to focus on the problem. So, instead of dealing with the problem and making it smaller, you don't deal with it, and it looms larger. Second, physical symptoms of stress begin to develop: you start to feel vaguely ill. Nobody wants to feel ill; it just adds to the worry! To restore your normal health, you need to break these vicious circles, and this book will show you just how this can be done.

RIGHT *Exercise and sunshine will help you to reduce stress and become healthy.*

for the future; it becomes impossible to get a problem out of your head; you find it difficult to relax, especially at night. Sometimes, stress can even make you slow down and become depressed, rather than agitated.

STRESS IS A PRIMITIVE RESPONSE

The way our bodies react to the mental pressures of modern-day life springs from the primitive human response to physical threat.

Human beings evolved as hunter-gatherers over the course of more than a million years, living first in the forests and then on the great savannas of Africa. The main threats to human survival were finding enough food and protecting ourselves from wild animals. We are not faced with the same physical threats in our lives today; they have been replaced by mental challenges – for example, family, work, finance, worries about our health. However, we have not had time to evolve a more appropriate way of responding to the new challenges: we still seem to respond to modern threats with the responses of the primitive human being! We need to look at those primitive responses to understand how we react to stress.

ABOVE *Primitive man had different threats.*

BELOW *Now we live in a concrete jungle.*

10

FIGHT OR FLIGHT

Imagine a primitive man faced by a hungry lion. He needs to react in a way that gives him the best chance of survival, to fight or to flee. There are four separate parts to this "fight or flight" reaction:

ABOVE *Something unexpected happens.*

ABOVE *You react immediately.*

ABOVE *The body responds instinctively.*

His fear is an automatic response in structures near the base of the brain, called the limbic system. Fear is the basic response that produces the other reactions.

He becomes mentally alert, active. Every nerve in the body is taut. This arousal happens deep inside the brain, in an area called the brain stem – close to the limbic system. He can learn new responses very swiftly. He can make decisions quickly, too.

His muscles need to be in a perfect state of readiness to fight or escape. Muscle tension is increased, making the spine rigid and the limbs stiff and powerful. This is under the control of the brain stem, too.

The internal functions of his body change to meet the threat. These are under automatic, unconscious control from the brain stem, acting through nerves called the autonomics. We shall look at these automatic changes next.

THE AUTONOMIC NERVES

The brain stem needs to be able to control the bodily functions so that they respond to potential danger (such as the threat from a lion). It does this automatically through the sympathetic nerves that speed the body up. The sympathetic nerves affect the circulation, accelerating the heart and redirecting blood toward the muscles. They also open up the lungs, increase sweat production to get rid of excess heat, and dilate the pupils. They even stimulate the bladder and bowels to empty themselves (to save carrying unnecessary weight). In all these ways, primitive man is preparing for fight or flight!

HORMONE ACTION

At the same time as the sympathetic nerves are active, the adrenal gland is stimulated to secrete adrenalin into the bloodstream. Adrenalin reinforces the effect of the sympathetic nerves on the heart and increases the supply of energy by releasing sugar stored in the liver. The response of the sympathetic nerves and adrenalin is virtually instantaneous. However, it is not very long-lasting. To continue the response to the threat, the adrenal gland functions to release cortisol, which has a much longer time period of action compared to adrenalin, taking an hour to start and continuing for several hours. It mobilizes energy from stores in various tissues and muscles.

HEIGHTENED SENSATIONS

The nerves that bring the sensations from the body to the brain pass through the brain stem; when it is activated, the sensations can be distorted or amplified. This heightened awareness was useful for primitive man, but today it serves no useful purpose; stressed people feel bodily sensations more acutely.

CONTROLLING THE BRAIN STEM

Although these activities of the brain stem operate unconsciously, it doesn't mean that we cannot influence them at all. It is important to realize that the brain stem responds to what is going on in the body, and you will learn how to quieten the brain stem down as part of your stress management.

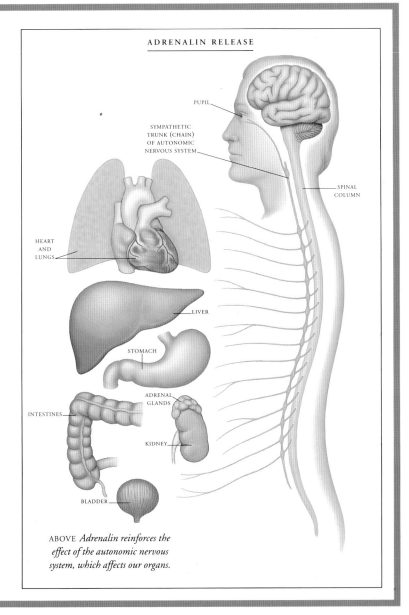

ADRENALIN RELEASE

PUPIL

SYMPATHETIC
TRUNK (CHAIN)
OF AUTONOMIC
NERVOUS SYSTEM

SPINAL
COLUMN

HEART
AND
LUNGS

LIVER

STOMACH

ADRENAL
GLANDS

INTESTINES

KIDNEY

BLADDER

ABOVE *Adrenalin reinforces the effect of the autonomic nervous system, which affects our organs.*

SYMPTOMS OF STRESS

Although we still respond mentally like primitive humans to the threats of modern life, with fear, agitation, and so on, we do not respond physically – we do not need "fight or flight" reactions. So all the extra energy and agitation remains pent up inside us, like a coiled spring.

HEALTH WARNING!

In the following pages we will take a look at the wide range of symptoms caused by stress. If you are already an anxious person, then you are very likely to search for these symptoms in yourself. They are quite likely to be there, previously unnoticed. And, if you notice a new symptom, you may start to worry about it. This is the vicious circle that makes your stress worse! The only reason to include this list of symptoms is so that you accept that they are all a normal part of the stress, and not signs of serious physical illness. Please do not go searching for symptoms that you have not already found: count yourself lucky and move on to the next one.

FEAR

A fundamental feeling in everyone who is stressed is an ill-defined fear for the future, that something dreadful is going to happen. It has been described as "fear spread out thin." It is probably not fear about any one thing, but is "free floating," i.e. ready to latch onto any new worry, such as another symptom, for example.

BELOW *Stress can cause confusion and fear.*

AGITATION

ABOVE *Stress at work can be infectious.*

A stressed person is highly agitated, vigilant, looking around all the time for new threats. They jump at sudden noises or movements. New ideas make a much more powerful impact than usual. Everything new seems to be too important, and they often feel it is overwhelmingly dangerous. It is difficult to get things in balance until the stress has settled. We have already seen how bodily sensations are amplified by the overactivity of the brain stem. This seems to apply particularly to feelings of warmth, which you may feel anywhere in the body, particularly rising up over the abdomen.

There is also a continuous restlessness that makes it difficult for the stressed person to sit in peace and quiet. One very common result of this mental agitation is insomnia, either difficulty getting off to sleep, or else waking up in the night and finding it hard to settle again. People sometimes experience feelings of unreality, or detachment.

STRESS IS CATCHING

Another remarkable thing about agitation is how infectious it is! People who are always "flying around," chasing their tails at work, seem to create the same sort of sense of urgency and stress in colleagues.

MUSCLE TENSION

This tension can affect muscles in any and every part of your body.

Scalp – headaches, worried frowning.
Face – worry lines.

✧

Throat – voice sounds high-pitched and breathless, feeling of lump in throat.
Jaws – teeth grinding at night; headaches.

✧

Around the eyes – squinting, frequent blinking.

Neck and shoulders – hunched shoulders, headache, stiff neck, head pushed forward.

✧

Forearm and hand – tennis elbow, tight grip (on steering wheel, white knuckles).

✧

Chest and abdomen – cannot breathe in deeply, feel short of breath.

✧

Back – backache
Legs and feet – cramps in legs and toes.

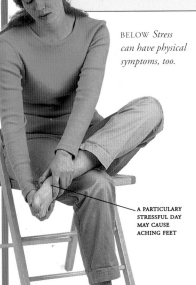

BELOW *Stress can have physical symptoms, too.*

A PARTICULARLY STRESSFUL DAY MAY CAUSE ACHING FEET

TREMOR, FATIGUE

Constant tension in your muscles may produce a continuous fine tremor. This can be most noticeable when you hold a cup and saucer. All this unremitting, excessive muscular effort drains the body and limbs of energy. It is usual for stressed people to feel tired, at least at the end of the day if not all the time. This can cause a feeling of lethargy and fatigue, which is sometimes so strong that it hides the excess agitation.

AUTONOMIC NERVES

ABOVE *You may have difficulty breathing regularly.*

The activity of the sympathetic nervous system is most noticeable in your heart and circulation, as your body is prepared for instant action:

● *Heart – beats faster and harder, increasing the circulation of blood.*

● *Pounding sensation in your chest.*

● *Pumping feeling in the neck.*

● *Rushing sound in the ears as the blood is pumped up to the brain.*

● *Palpitations – the heart rate may be irregular as it seems to trip over itself.*

● *Blood pressure – often raised in people who are stressed, but it rarely produces any symptoms (although most people think that raised blood pressure causes headaches); identified only when it is measured in the arm.*

OTHER SYMPTOMS OF SYMPATHETIC ACTIVITY INCLUDE

✧ Sweating, especially the palms

✧ Cold skin, especially hands and feet

✧ Dizziness

✧ Overactivity of the stomach and bowel – increased noises from the intestines, flatus (gas) and diarrhea; abdomen often feels distended (this combination is often called "irritable bowel syndrome," but the name only hides the basic cause, which is stress).

✧ Appetite is usually poor, because of nausea.

✧ Some people notice they eat more when stressed for comfort.

✧ There is increased frequency of passing urine.

RIGHT *Up to 20 percent of new mothers experience stress.*

17

RECOGNIZING STRESSED BEHAVIOR

There are a number of tell-tale signs that someone is stressed, ranging from body language to concentration levels.

One of the first giveaway signs that someone is stressed is a cold, sweaty handshake. People under stress typically sit on the edge of the chair, looking stiff and agitated. They become over-talkative with a high pitched voice, and perhaps a repeated, nervous laugh. They may not listen to people they are talking with, but instead follow their own trains of thoughts and anxieties. They wring their hands, impatiently tap their fingers or feet, or play nervously with a pen. Their movements are hasty, and they are liable to be clumsy and have minor accidents.

ABOVE *Anxious people may eat greedily or not at all.*

EATING PROBLEMS

Most people under stress lose their appetite and lose weight. They may look thin, as well as tired and drawn. They may pick at food, or alternatively gobble down candy and cookies.

LACK OF CONCENTRATION

The restlessness makes it difficult for them to concentrate on one thing. They may have difficulty applying themselves to the day's work and may

change the subject of a conversation aimlessly. They may find themselves unable to relax or to enjoy sex (this often applies to men, who may become anxious about their performance).

ABOVE *Caffeine can add to stress.*

UNDERLYING ANGER

People who are normally dynamic may become frustrated by overwork or insoluble problems at home and develop a sense of frustration. This can erupt as swearing, temper tantrums, and even physical violence. They may display an underlying hostility to everybody around them.

DRUG DEPENDENCY

People who habitually use drugs, such as caffeine, nicotine, or alcohol, typically find themselves using these crutches more and more as stress creeps up on them. These drugs themselves produce side effects that we will be looking at later.

HURRY SICKNESS

People who are high achievers and are under stress often display a pattern of behavior called "hurry sickness." They rush impetuously at all new tasks; they often do two things at once to save time; when things aren't happening, they tap their fingers or their pens; they are impatient with anyone who talks slowly or thoughtfully, and so they constantly interrupt or finish sentences for them; they rush up the stairs two at a time; they become frantic if they are delayed by traffic jams or have to stop at traffic lights. They even brush their teeth ferociously.

BELOW *Stress may surface in the home with displays of temper.*

DIFFERENT FORMS OF STRESS

We shall now look at how stress can affect people in different ways. It is normal to experience some features of more than one type of stress reaction.

NORMAL STRESS REACTIONS

Problems in the family or with money, work, or health are bound to make you anxious; it is only natural. The anxiety will usually be in proportion to the severity of the problem, and will fade away within a few weeks, particularly if the problem itself is resolved. More severe life changes, such as divorce, bereavement, or redundancy, often produce a mixture of anxiety, depression, and irritability over the following weeks or months. Again, this reaction is entirely understandable and fades with time as you gradually come to terms with the loss. This often takes 6 to 12 months or longer. These changes leave emotional scars, of course. If you think your reaction is extreme, you may need to discuss it with your physician.

GENERALIZED ANXIETY DISORDER

If your stress reaction is excessive and out of proportion to the problem, you may be suffering from what is called generalized anxiety disorder. The essential feature of this condition is extreme worry.

LEFT *Money – or lack of it – is often a cause of anxiety.*

ANXIETY CHECKLIST

Ask yourself the following questions:

1 *Do you believe that your worry is excessively severe considering your problems?*

2 *Has your worry been going on for more than six months?*

3 *Does your worry concern at least two everyday events or problems of life?*

4 *Is your worry noticeable for more than half of every day?*

5 *Do you have negative thoughts that intrude more than usual? (such as "When will I ever be better?"), and are they more difficult to drive out than usual?*

If your answer to any of the questions above is an honest "no," the advice in this book should be enough to help you manage the problems. If your answer is "yes" to all questions, then you may consider looking for additional help in learning how to handle the stress.

BELOW *If you are prone to stress, do not suffer alone – seek professional advice.*

WHO IS AFFECTED BY GENERALIZED ANXIETY DISORDER?

Generalized anxiety disorder commonly starts some time in the 20s, but it may occur at any time, in response to stress factors, up to the 40s, rarely later. It affects men and women in equal numbers. It is a common condition, probably involving around 2 to 5 percent of the population and accounting for about 30 percent of a family physician's consultations.

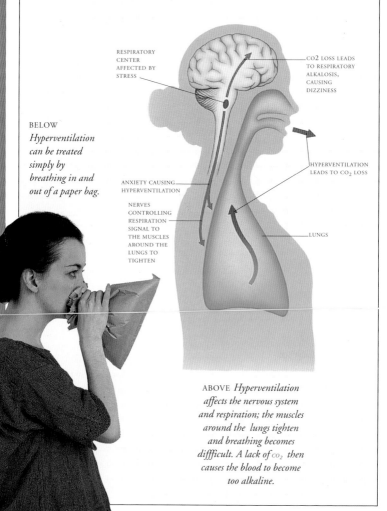

TREATING HYPERVENTILATION

RESPIRATORY CENTER AFFECTED BY STRESS

CO2 LOSS LEADS TO RESPIRATORY ALKALOSIS, CAUSING DIZZINESS

HYPERVENTILATION LEADS TO CO_2 LOSS

ANXIETY CAUSING HYPERVENTILATION

NERVES CONTROLLING RESPIRATION SIGNAL TO THE MUSCLES AROUND THE LUNGS TO TIGHTEN

LUNGS

BELOW
Hyperventilation can be treated simply by breathing in and out of a paper bag.

ABOVE *Hyperventilation affects the nervous system and respiration; the muscles around the lungs tighten and breathing becomes diffficult. A lack of CO_2 then causes the blood to become too alkaline.*

22

BURNOUT

This term is used to describe the emotional blunting and lack of initiative that is felt by people who have suffered prolonged, untreated stress. It is a poor word because it implies that the condition is final and cannot be treated, which is not true. It simply requires good stress management, carefully practiced for a prolonged period.

ABOVE *Do not use a plastic bag for breathing exercises.*

HYPERVENTILATION

Stress causes tension in the muscles between and around the ribs that are involved in breathing. The muscle tension feels rather like when you are out of breath after running for a bus. But you are breathing normally, not rapidly. Surely something is wrong? You find yourself making a conscious effort to breathe.

But you don't actually need to make this effort – there's nothing wrong with your breathing, only with the muscles. So you are now breathing too fast. That doesn't bring any extra oxygen into the blood, which is already full of oxygen, but does drive out the little bit of carbon dioxide. You need that carbon dioxide, which keeps the blood in balance, so you now start to feel faint and dizzy. This is worrying, so your chest muscles tighten a bit more, and you try to breathe harder. This upsets the balance of calcium in the blood, so your nerves and muscles become more twitchy. You start to feel tingling in the fingers and feet, and eventually spasm of the muscles. You are hyperventilating.

Fortunately, this is one condition that responds immediately to a simple treatment: put a paper bag over your mouth and nose, and breathe gently in and out of the bag. (Do NOT use a plastic bag!) Your symptoms will melt away. You must prevent future attacks by becoming aware of your breathing and your muscle tension, as described in detail later.

PANIC ATTACKS

Panic attacks are quite common and are experienced by 1 out of 50 women and 1 out of 100 men. They can start out of the blue, even while you are asleep. You may feel an overwhelming sense of impending disaster or death, or feel you are "going crazy." You usually feel dizzy and faint, choke, and have difficulty breathing. You may experience a feeling of being smothered, tightness of the chest, "pounding heart," trembling, butterflies in the stomach, or tingling in the fingers. All these reactions seem to occur for no reason.

You may be rushed to the hospital emergency room, only to be told that there is nothing wrong; so why do you feel so awful? Fortunately, panic attacks like this fade away within an hour or two, leaving you bewildered but relieved.

RIGHT *Panic attacks can strike at any time; they give a sense of intense fear or "craziness".*

ABOVE *You may feel as jittery as a butterfly.*

DIZZINESS

DIFFICULTY BREATHING

FEEL CHOKED AND TRAPPED

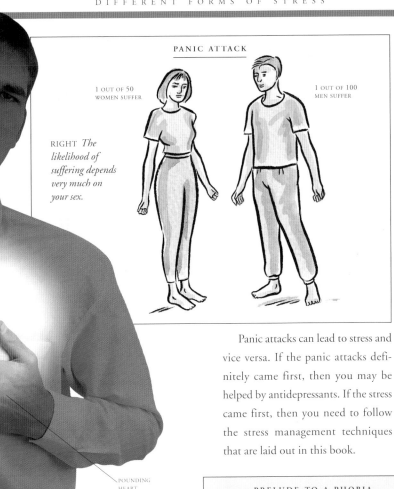

PANIC ATTACK

1 OUT OF 50
WOMEN SUFFER

1 OUT OF 100
MEN SUFFER

RIGHT *The likelihood of suffering depends very much on your sex.*

POUNDING
HEART

STOMACH
UPSET

Panic attacks can lead to stress and vice versa. If the panic attacks definitely came first, then you may be helped by antidepressants. If the stress came first, then you need to follow the stress management techniques that are laid out in this book.

PRELUDE TO A PHOBIA

After a panic attack, you may believe that it was caused by what was going on at the time, or the place where you were. So you will tend to avoid those particular circumstances in future. This is how phobias develop.

AGORAPHOBIA

Agoraphobia usually starts between the ages of 15 and 35. It is at least twice as common in women as men. The worst part is feeling trapped, unable to escape, and not having help available. The word agoraphobia means "Fear of the marketplace," originally referring to the busy market at the center of ancient Greek cities, crowded with traders, shoppers, politicians, and philosophers all in heated debate. (The modern equivalent is the line in the supermarket!)

HOW DOES IT START?

Exhausted by the hard work of shopping, trying to cope with children, perhaps dressed too warmly in the hot and airless supermarket, standing in line is enough to make anyone feel dizzy and faint. The whole thing is made worse by the fear of making a spectacle of yourself. You feel frightened, which only makes the symptoms worse. This vicious circle may lead to an attack of hyperventilation or panic. Escape from the supermarket into the cool outside brings a feeling of enormous relief.

THE PHOBIA TAKES HOLD

The fear of this happening again is terrifying, so it is not surprising that you will be reluctant to visit that supermarket again. You will probably be afraid to visit any other supermarket, in case the same thing might happen. If you are experiencing these symptoms you are developing

LEFT *Crowds of people cause a lot of distress to agoraphobics.*

agoraphobia. There are now special methods for treating agoraphobia.

Other situations where you may develop a fear that you cannot escape, or where help is unavailable, include: elevators, bridges, being alone at home, crowds, and public transportation. All these are included in the same term – agoraphobia.

OTHER PHOBIAS

As much as 9 percent of the population are known to suffer from severe stress or a phobia that is set off by a specific situation or object – such as a hypodermic needle. It may start when you are told about a danger in a dramatic way – or suddenly exposed to the situation. Phobias need specialized help, which is often successful.

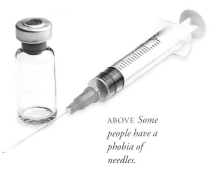

ABOVE *Some people have a phobia of needles.*

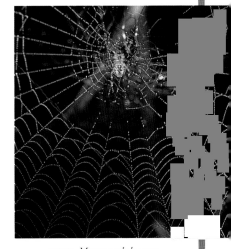

ABOVE *Many people have an inexplicable fear of spiders and cannot bear to see them.*

SOCIAL PHOBIA

Social phobia probably affects about 2 percent of people. It is normal to feel some discomfort when you are being stared at, for example, making a speech in public, meeting people, eating in public. In social phobia, this discomfort becomes a marked fear of embarrassment or humiliation. It is more than just shyness or personal insecurity, and can be so marked that it makes you avoid the situation, interfering with your normal life.

STRESS AND YOUR PHYSICIAN

Because of all the symptoms anxiety causes, advice from a knowledgeable professional will often be useful. The ideal person is a family physician who understands stress and recognizes the need for advice and guidance in decisions about prescribed drugs or referral to a specialist, when necessary.

Physicians know that patients are generally anxious about coming to see them, particularly when a condition is newly diagnosed. They will not cause extra anxiety by careless use of words that are commonly misunderstood; "chronic," for example, means "severe" to most people, but to physicians it simply means that an illness has been going on for more than three months. It is now well recognized that stress makes all medical conditions feel worse; whatever the problem, dealing with the accompanying stress is the key to managing pain and other unpleasant symptoms.

ABOVE *Even going to the physician to discuss stress can be a cause of anxiety in itself.*

IS IT STRESS, OR SOMETHING ELSE?

Occasionally, symptoms that seem to be stress are caused by other medical conditions. In thyrotoxicosis, the thyroid gland in the neck becomes overactive. This can cause a tremor, fast pulse, palpitations, sweating, and increased mental activity. It can usually be distinguished from stress by blood tests. Other, much rarer, conditions can lead to the release of excess amounts of hormones such as adrenalin into the bloodstream. The symptoms are clearly intermittent, and you would feel all right in between attacks.

Some mental conditions produce anxiety as well as their main symptoms, such as hearing voices, finding one's thoughts disordered, or becoming obsessional (such as excessive handwashing or cleaning the house). If this is the case, a medical opinion is needed as other treatment is likely to be more appropriate.

CHEMICAL CAUSES OF STRESS

Changes in hormones (the body's own chemicals) are known to make some people vulnerable to stress: two examples are pre-menstrual tension and the post-menopausal syndrome.

Excessive use of stimulants may also be confused with stress. Caffeine or nicotine toxicity gradually build up as the drug accumulates over weeks of overuse. Both of these stimulants can cause tremor, sleep disturbance, dizziness, tight chest with breathlessness, and fatigue – just like stress. The obvious answer is to stop taking the stimulant drug, or at least to lower the intake. Note, however, that suddenly reducing caffeine intake may cause headaches two to three days later.

Agitation can also be caused by withdrawal from drugs that suppress the nervous system, such as alcohol. Sudden withdrawal produces agitation, fast pulse with palpitations, sweating, insomnia. Withdrawal from illegal drugs, particularly the heroin and morphine group, also produces a state of anxiety and again requires specialized help.

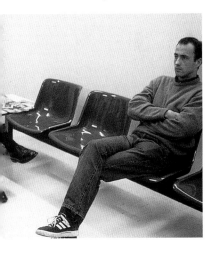

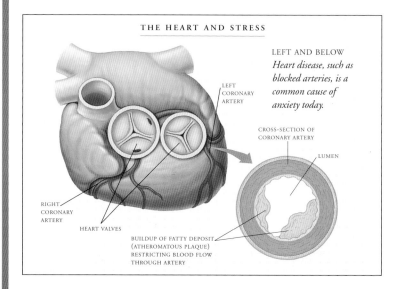

THE HEART AND STRESS

LEFT CORONARY ARTERY

LEFT AND BELOW
*Heart disease, such as
blocked arteries, is a
common cause of
anxiety today.*

CROSS-SECTION OF
CORONARY ARTERY

LUMEN

RIGHT CORONARY ARTERY

HEART VALVES

BUILDUP OF FATTY DEPOSIT
(ATHEROMATOUS PLAQUE)
RESTRICTING BLOOD FLOW
THROUGH ARTERY

ANXIETY AND
THE HEART

We have seen that muscle tension can cause chest pain and palpitations. This is not due to heart disease and does not cause heart disease, though of course it is possible that heart disease is present as well. It should be excluded by the physician by all reasonable means. If the symptoms of stress are present anyway, the wise physician will address them with the patient immediately, without waiting to see the result of special tests.

Heart disease makes people very anxious. The heart is so obviously fundamental to life, and heart disease is so common in the industrialized Western world, that most people will know somebody who has died from it. However, sometimes this fear is out of all proportion to the actual severity of the disease. People can become incapacitated even though their disease is minor: they lose confidence and place severe restrictions on themselves and their lifestyles in order to protect themselves, when in fact there is no need.

OTHER CONDITIONS AGGRAVATED BY STRESS

People with conditions that come and go, such as asthma, eczema, migraine, and some stomach and bowel conditions, will already know that their condition is often made worse by stress. Research has shown that effectively dealing with the stress can reduce the frequency of attacks. The relationship between stress and other diseases is less certain. It has been suggested by some people that stress can affect the activity of the immune system, but the evidence that has been presented so far is not entirely convincing.

RIGHT *Certain techniques – such as listening to your favorite song – may reduce bouts of stress.*

PHYSICIAN DEPENDENCY

Physicians are obviously in a powerful position to reassure patients about their symptoms. This leads to a rapid relief of anxiety, which is satisfying for both patient and physician. This relief is very rewarding and is in many ways a good thing. Next time the stressed patient develops symptoms, he or she will not wait so long before seeing the physician, to experience that sense of relief once more. This can rapidly lead to a situation where the patient becomes dependent on the physician, with increasingly frequent visits to the physician for trivial complaints. The patient finds it easier to be reassured by the physician, rather than to recognize the underlying stress for themselves and deal with it appropriately.

WORRYING ABOUT SYMPTOMS

A particularly common and fundamental reaction to stress is hypochondria, a form of morbid depression that is caused by unnecessary anxiety about health.

People who are hypochondriacal are often looked down upon by other people, including physicians, because they feel unable to help. This attitude is totally wrong and fundamentally misunderstands the whole process of anxiety. It is crucial that you recognize the basic fear of disease underlying your symptoms. Only by understanding and facing up to it will you restore a healthy attitude to your body.

WHAT HAPPENS?

We have already seen that stress produces bodily symptoms, usually symptoms that haven't been experienced before. These symptoms are of course experienced in the brain, and they reach the feeling part of the brain (cortex) by passing directly through the brain stem. But we have already established that the brain stem is frantically overactive in stress.

RIGHT *Hypochondria and general fear of illness may be a symptom of stress.*

RIGHT *Hypochondriacs often have a wide selection of pills and medicines.*

VITAMIN PILLS

ANTIBIOTIC PILLS

Therefore, your brain will inevitably pay extra attention to these new symptoms. And since your brain is in a state of free-floating fear, almost looking for something to worry about, it will inevitably become frightened at these new symptoms. It therefore interprets them as signs of serious underlying disease. Understanding this natural progression will allow you to begin to control it.

"I know in my heart of hearts there can't be anything serious because I am still here. But I can't stop being terrified."

You feel ill, but you know you are not. This conflict undermines your self-confidence. And it doesn't help very much to be reassured by the physician that there's no sign of serious illness. It is the stress that needs to be addressed.

PLANNING SELF-HELP

You should by now have a good understanding of how
stress affects the body. The rest of this book will describe
many ways in which you can manage your stress.

We recommend that you start your self-help program immediately with the "basic techniques" suggested below, to reduce the effects of stress on your body and mind. Then you'll be ready to look at the stress factors.

POSITIVE THINKING

You may have become demoralized by the apparent lack of active help. But you have already demonstrated that you are motivated: after all, you're still reading this book! How can you keep your

1. BE YOUR OWN THERAPIST: BASIC TECHNIQUES

✧ Start working to increase your stress resistance by improving your lifestyle and temperament.

✧ Begin to control your breathing and relax muscle tension.

These are the basic techniques that everyone needs.

ABOVE *Turn over a new leaf and set yourself goals like getting into shape.*

2. BE YOUR OWN THERAPIST: COMPLEMENTARY TECHNIQUES

✧ Other methods and techniques will be described that will help you with muscle tension and autonomic activity and to calm the mind directly. You can choose any of these that seem appropriate to your circumstances and outlook.

motivation? You could write down some of your worst thoughts and feelings of the last few days or weeks. In a month's time, look back at that record and see how much better you are.

STAY FIRM

Don't forget that you may be open to influence from other people. Now you are determined to get better, so don't let anyone deter you. Keep away from the "doom-merchants" and anyone else who is terribly stressed. (If you want to help

them, you can do this later when you have conquered stress yourself.) Surround yourself with positive things: calm, restorative surroundings, pleasant music, and, most important, good reliable friends.

THE BRAIN

STIMULATION OF HIGHER CENTERS

RETICULAR ACTIVATING SYSTEM

SPINAL CORD

SYMPATHETIC NERVOUS SYSTEM TRIGGERS PHYSICAL SYMPTOMS

ABOVE *If the brain is overstimulated and stressed, it will cause physical symptoms that may need medical treatment.*

3. LOOKING AT YOUR STRESS FACTORS

❖ By now, you will be ready to start looking at the causes of stress. As you will be less stressed, you will be able to see things in context.

❖ If you need to make changes, you will not rush into decisions that you may later regret.

4. THE STRESSED MIND

❖ This is where to look if you need stronger treatment, whether you are working with specialized therapists or taking prescribed medicines.

INCREASING STRESS RESISTANCE

There are two ways you can increase your strength
to resist stress – through making changes to your
lifestyle and your temperament.

LIFESTYLE

Lifestyle changes sound difficult and boring! But nobody is asking you to stop having fun, and our grandmothers' saying is still true: "Laughter is the best medicine."

LEFT
*Smile and you
will reduce stress.*

TIME AND SPACE

When did you last sit down, take time for yourself, and give yourself space? At work or at home, you may always be chasing deadlines and targets or meeting other people's needs. "Time off" is vital and actually allows you to meet the demands more effectively. Although it may seem counterproductive to stop and sit down when you're hectically busy, try stopping just to unwind for a minute: it can be therapeutic and make you more efficient. Watching an aquarium or listening to music can help. Nobody can keep working at 110 percent capacity all the time. You need proper breaks for weekends and vacations, and the chance to get away to restore your balance and composure. Some people find the country or the coast particularly relaxing.

RIGHT *Spending time outdoors improving your health is always beneficial.*

HOBBIES AND PASTIMES

These can be very powerful ways of diverting attention from your difficulties. Try meeting people from different walks of life, who may have a calming influence, especially if they are involved in creative pursuits (such as music, art, drama) or physical activity (hiking). Joining clubs offers friendship and social support that increases our self-esteem.

MOVEMENT

Humans were not designed to be couch potatoes, but to be up and about. Exercise has a powerful part to play in dealing with stress.

RELIGION

There is no doubt that belief in a personal God can help people with stress in many different ways. However, beware of any religion that appears to be based on one charismatic individual, which insists that its members isolate themselves from ordinary life and particularly from their families.

MONEY

Money is often quoted as a source of stress, by rich and poor alike! Poverty alone has been shown not to be a cause of stress (although it can make fighting stress more tricky, through lack of resources).

LEFT *New hobbies are often suggested to people who are overworked.*

ABOVE *Sitting down to eat, instead of eating on the go, is restful.*

EATING

It is important to say that worrying about food too much seems to cause more problems than it ever solves. The overall aim must be to eat a varied and nutritious diet, without undue haste. If this describes you already, there is no need to read on.

FOOD SENSITIVITY

Stress is often blamed on a food sensitivity, an overwhelming candidiasis (an infection from a yeast organism), or some nutritional deficiency. There

is in fact very little evidence for any of these causes: genuine food sensitivities are really very rare; overwhelming candida infection only affects people who are already seriously ill; and a varied Western diet is rarely deficient in anything.

EATING AT THE RIGHT PACE

On the other hand, it does matter how you eat. Part of the merry-go-round of stress is that you feel too busy to stop, so you rush your food. Now, you may have noticed that eating makes you feel slower and calmer, with a sense of well-being. This may be due to the release of certain chemicals (endorphins) within the brain. And the quicker you fill your stomach, the stronger these feelings are. So you may choose sweet, highly refined food, such as cookies, since they can be eaten more quickly. But these foods do not contain any fiber, so the stomach does not remain full for long. The comforting effect soon wears off, and you need to eat again – and you probably will choose more cookies! This urge for sweet things is sometimes explained as hypoglycemia, or low blood sugar; in fact, hypoglycemia is very rare in normal healthy people. The empty stomach theory is a much more likely explanation. So, if you find you eat too fast, choose foods with a high fiber content so you have to eat them more slowly; the calming effect may not be so rapid, but it will last, without any rebound hunger pangs.

ABOVE *Healthy eating including plenty of fresh fruit can make a difference.*

SMOKING

Smoking stimulates and calms you, but when the effect of the nicotine wears off, you feel agitated again. People who smoke are in a bind: they cannot do without it, but they know it makes them worse. Stopping should be part of the recovery plan. Meanwhile, set yourself a strict daily limit, and stick to it.

ALCOHOL

Alcohol is also a mixed blessing for stress. A little can help you relax; but it is absolutely clear that regular alcohol actually increases stress. Stick to one or two units at most, have two days a week without alcohol, and you can feel sure you will not be any worse.

ABOVE *A little alcohol on occasion is harmless.*

STRESS-PRONE TEMPERAMENTS

There are certain temperaments or personality types that are known to have lower resistance to stress. Our personalities grow up with us and develop as a result of external and internal influences. It is

ABOVE *Stress can lead to hostility and even provocation.*

not easy to make major changes in temperament without a good deal of expert professional help. However, if you can identify any of these traits in yourself and try to behave differently every time you catch yourself up to your old habits, you could do yourself a lot of good.

HIGHLY COMPETITIVE

The temperament in which individuals are highly competitive, hard-driving, impatient, and rather inflexible is well recognized. Some people with this personality manage to retain a sense of proportion in their work and are high achievers. Others develop a

semipermanent state of stress that is marked by hostility and anger. They show all the hallmarks of the hurry sickness, described earlier, and they cannot relax without feeling guilty. They often cannot recognize the value of other people.

Action to take: Make a conscious effort to identify and deal with your haste and hostility. For example, if you race through red traffic lights, then punish yourself by going around the block so

you have to pass through the same lights again; if they are red again, stop and calm yourself down with some breathing exercises (see pages 42–7).

PERFECTIONIST

Some people are obsessed by producing order and perfection, and become distressed if they are forced into a situation of chaos and compromise. Such people are rather rigid and inflexible, and tend to be sticklers for time-keeping. Their entire lives have to be planned meticulously, and they tend to include the lives of people around them. Normal life is frequently not perfect and may produce feelings of stress.

Action to take: Identifying aspects of your rigid behavior may allow you to see how it can be modified in a way that can be regarded as a balance and not a sell-out to your principles.

LEFT *Some personalities try to juggle everything at once.*

OVER-IDENTIFICATION

Some people set a lot of store by their work status. Achievements at work do lead to increased self-esteem, but over-identification can cause problems if it dominates your life to the detriment of your leisure interests and makes you vulnerable to criticism.

Action to take: Look at ways of developing interests outside work.

ABOVE *Status means everything to some people.*

A BORN WORRIER?

In these days, when everything seems to be ruled by our genes, it is interesting to find that anxiety is not inherited. Nobody is a "born" worrier! On the other hand, you may be prone to stress because of events in the past, such as being separated too early from your mother, or being abused in childhood. If you identify emotions from such events, you may benefit from good professional help through your doctor. Otherwise, there is little point in dwelling on the past, it is much better to get on with doing something about the present for the sake of the future, following the advice given here.

BREATH CONTROL AND MUSCLE RELAXATION

In this key section, we shall be introducing two procedures that everyone can use safely, and that can have profound effects on the body and the autonomic nerves, thereby reducing stress.

As we have seen, both breathing and muscular tension are under unconscious control from the brain-stem: stress increases them both. The brain stem in turn receives information from lungs and muscles, called feedback. Tense breathing or tense muscles make the brain stem agitated (yet another vicious circle of stress!)

The important thing is this: you can control both your breathing and your muscular tension consciously. With a little practice, you can learn to calm down your brain stem!

PRACTICE

Breath control and muscle relaxation are not difficult procedures to learn or practice, even if you have never done anything like it before. Plan to spend ten minutes twice a day regularly: do not be overambitious at first and then find you cannot maintain the practice. Time yourself with a watch. Start with breath control, and as soon as you are able, add muscle relaxation exercise to your routine.

RIGHT *Try and plan to spend ten minutes each day practicing breath control.*

USEFUL STANDBY

As you gain experience, you will also be able to use both techniques throughout the day, and in whatever position you want, sitting, standing, or walking. They are a powerful first-aid procedure to use whenever you face a stressful situation, whether it be a colleague challenging you at work, children arguing, or a hot and over-crowded supermarket.

SELF-MONITORING

Learning breath control and muscle relaxation teaches you to become aware of what is happening from moment to moment with your breathing and your muscle tension, and in this way you can monitor your current state of stress.

EVIDENCE

There is good, clear scientific evidence that breath control and muscular relaxation are safe and effective ways of reducing anxiety. This has been shown for people who are anxious

ABOVE *Relief from stress can make the world seem like a new place again.*

already, as well as people who have to undergo hospital treatment. Breath control and muscular relaxation reduce the body's response to stress, mainly by lowering the pulse and blood pressure. They help significantly in rehabilitation, for example after suffering a coronary thrombosis. They are even strong enough to help stress from hormonal causes – for example, during menopause. There is also every reason to believe they are just as effective for relieving premenstrual tension.

RIGHT *Finding time to practice muscle relaxation is essential.*

DIFFERENT FORMS OF BREATHING

Before putting breath control into practice, it is best to know something about the different ways of breathing, so that you can identify your own pattern.

DIAPHRAGM BREATHING

If you have ever had the opportunity of watching a newborn baby, you will have noticed that its abdomen is going in and out smoothly and regularly. It appears to be breathing with its stomach! But the muscles of the abdomen are soft: it is not those, but the diaphragm muscle, that is doing the work (see diagram, far right). Breathing with the diaphragm is the most efficient way of getting the required oxygen into the body and expelling the carbon dioxide. We can breathe like this all day without getting the least bit tired!

CHEST BREATHING

This form of breathing takes over when an individual is out of breath through exercise – or is under stress. It uses the muscles between the ribs. Often during chest breathing, the abdomen is sucked in because the diaphragm has been pulled up by the work of the chest muscles. This is inefficient. In "civilized" societies, most people start chest breathing before adulthood, probably due to stress. Re-educating yourself away from chest breathing is crucial.

LEFT *Breathlessness can cause panic and distress.*

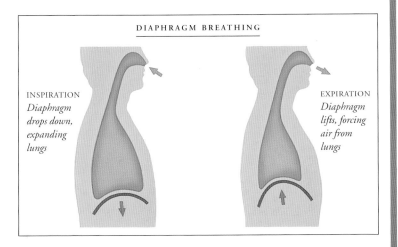

DIAPHRAGM BREATHING

INSPIRATION
*Diaphragm
drops down,
expanding
lungs*

EXPIRATION
*Diaphragm
lifts, forcing
air from
lungs*

ACCESSORY BREATHING

The third form of breathing occurs when an individual becomes more short of breath, either in lung conditions such as asthma or bronchitis, or in hyperventilation (see page 23). This form of breathing uses the accessory muscles as well as the chest muscles: the muscles of the neck and shoulders literally pull the shoulders upward, expanding the upper domes of the lungs. The additional lung capacity is actually very small. But, like chest breathing, the extra effort of the accessory muscles feeds back into the brain and causes agitation.

PARADOXICAL BREATHING

This problem usually only occurs if you have been stressed for a long time. The diaphragm and abdominal muscles contract together (as if to protect you from an anticipated punch), so that the whole trunk becomes rigid. This splints the lower part of the lungs, leading to greater effort of breathing and interfering with conversation: it is as if you are trying to talk while holding your breath.

The smooth rhythm of breathing in inspiration and expiration is very important. People who are stressed often breathe with deep sighs.

Find time and space to yourself where you will not be disturbed. Remove your shoes and loosen clothing around your neck, chest, and abdomen. Lie quietly on the floor with a pillow under your head and arms by your sides, palms upward.

EXERCISE 1:
BREATH CONTROL

1 *Identify when you are breathing in and when you are breathing out – use the back of your fingers to feel breath out through the nose.*

2 *Concentrate on steadying your breathing so that it is regular and slow.*

3 *Put a hand just below your ribs, in the middle. Most likely, as you breathe in, you will be pulling in the abdominal muscle and your hand will sink. This is chest breathing and your aim is to reverse it. Each time you breathe in, concentrate on using the breath to push the abdomen, and your hand, outwards. When you do this, you are using your diaphragm and breathing deeply and efficiently.*

4 *Your mind will inevitably wander from the breathing exercise at some point. This is quite natural. Just become aware of the thought and then shift your attention back to the breathing.*

5 *As with all exercises, when you have finished, roll onto your side and get up carefully to prevent dizziness.*

As you gain experience, you will be able to control your breathing very precisely so that both inspiration and expiration are slow and steady with hardly a gap between them. You can then start breath control in different positions, firstly sitting, then standing, walking, and so on.

LEFT *Find somewhere peaceful before lying quietly on the floor.*

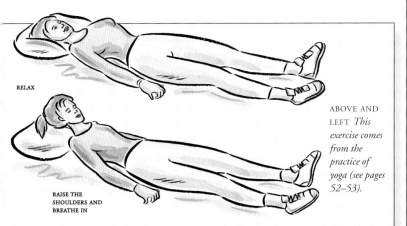

RELAX

RAISE THE
SHOULDERS AND
BREATHE IN

ABOVE AND
LEFT *This
exercise comes
from the
practice of
yoga (see pages
52–53).*

EXERCISE 2:
DEEP RELAXING BREATH

This is a Yoga breathing exercise, and will help you identify your patterns of breathing. It is useful to perform this three times at the beginning of a muscle relaxation exercise. Lie on the floor as above.

● *Breathe in, first allowing the abdomen to swell as much as possible; then continue to breathe in, expanding the ribs; finally continue to breathe in raising the shoulders with the neck and shoulder muscles. Then breathe out, smoothly and steadily. Repeat this twice.*

This exercise must not be hurried or it may make you feel dizzy. Count slowly to about four (depending how fit you are) for each section of the breath in and then breathe out.

RELAXED STANCE

If you are concerned about your posture, you may not like the idea of a floppy, relaxed abdomen when you stand up! Western culture thinks your abdomen should be flat, but more natural cultures let their abdomens protrude – and they don't get stressed! There is a way round this with the Alexander Technique (see pages 66–67).

There are different exercises to achieve muscle relaxation. The first one given here is useful if you cannot already recognize muscle tension; if you can, use the second one. It doesn't matter if you start with the head or the toes.

EXERCISE 1: TENSION-RELAXATION

RIGHT *Hunch your shoulders.*

1 *Find time and space to yourself, remove your shoes, and loosen any tight clothing. Lie in a straight line, heels slightly apart and feet flopping outward; place your arms by your sides, palms up, fingers relaxed, eyes closed.*

WARNING!

This exercise involves strong muscle contractions. There may be particular reasons (such as physical injury) why you may have to be careful in a particular part of your body.

2 *Tighten the muscles of the face, closing eyes, nose, and mouth all at once: count slowly to 5 and notice the muscle tension. When the tension is really marked, and you have counted to 5, suddenly let go of the tension: now become aware of the relaxation there. Repeat this process of tensing muscles and then suddenly releasing the tension, all over the body.*

3 *Hunch your shoulders up toward your ears as hard as possible.*

Repeat. Raising and tensing the left arm, form a tight fist. Repeat with the right arm.

4 *Tighten the muscles of the abdomen, hard like a board. Breathe out when you relax them.*

LEFT *Squeeze your eyes shut.*

ABOVE *Raise your left leg and tense all the muscles in it.*

5 *Raise the left leg, tensing the whole leg and pointing the toes hard at the wall beyond you. Repeat with the right leg.*

6 *Now turn your attention back over the body, concentrating on the face muscles, the neck and shoulder muscles, the arms, abdomen, and legs, checking that you are still completely relaxed and limp. Enjoy the feeling for the remainder of the 10 minutes you have set aside.*

7 *Open your eyes, take slightly deeper breaths, and turn on your side before getting up.*

RIGHT *Let the chair support you.*

EXERCISE 2:
DEEP RELAXATION

You can do this lying on a carpet or bed as before, or sitting in a comfortable chair with the neck and head supported, hands in the lap or on the thighs, palms up; legs uncrossed, feet flat on the floor, eyes closed.

1 *Become aware of the feet and legs below the knees: feel the tension in them, then let them relax, let them feel heavy and supported.*

2 *Move your attention to the thighs and knees: let them relax and feel heavy and supported.*

3 *Now repeat this throughout the body, working on your buttocks, back, abdomen, chest, shoulders, neck, scalp.*

4 *Enjoy the feeling of deep relaxation for 10 minutes before gently rousing yourself.*

COMPLEMENTARY STRESS CONTROL METHODS

Some of the following methods you can learn on your own; with others you will need some help. All of them will help you combat stress if you practice them on a regular basis (say twice daily). It is important to take the space and time for regular practice: give yourself the attention you deserve!

Once you have learned a technique, you will be able to use it whenever you need, for the rest of your life. So choose one that works for you.

GENTLE WARNINGS

Breathing and relaxation can be done safely by anyone, with care if you have physical problems. The mind therapies such as meditation and self-hypnosis are rather different: if you have a psychiatric history (previous breakdown, or been under the care of a psychiatrist or your doctor for any length of time for a mental problem),

you should seek advice before starting: meditation, for example, may make you feel disorientated or alienated from society.

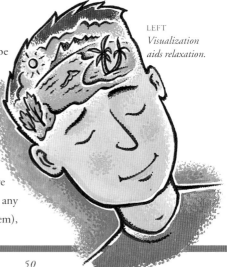

LEFT
Visualization aids relaxation.

Many of these therapies can produce short-term changes such as vivid dreams when you start, and you may become more emotional. These effects are not harmful, but you should know about them.

ABOVE *A biofeedback professional measures bodily electrical activity.*

As a general rule, for safety reasons, meditation and self-hypnosis should never be practiced for more than 20 minutes on each occasion, and never more than twice in the same day.

RIGHT *Try to be aware of the time when you are meditating.*

BIOFEEDBACK

Biofeedback aims at calming arousal in the brain stem by focusing attention on electrical measurement of one or other bodily activity. The activities that can be measured include muscle tension, skin resistance, which falls at times of stress, or the brain's own electrical signals, the EEG. Electrodes are placed on the skin in the appropriate place and connected to a box which either makes a sound or shines a light. The intensity of the sound or light varies with the body's electrical activity. By following various thoughts and concentrating on procedures, you discover that you can reduce the intensity of the sound or light signal. This reduces the arousal of your brain stem. It is usual to be taught biofeedback by a professional. Several good-quality scientific studies have shown that biofeedback can help reduce anxiety, and it works well with children.

YOGA

Yoga is an ancient Indian practice that has been adopted in the West for promoting health, and managing stress and conditions such as migraine, tension headaches, and asthma: there is evidence that it does work.

Yoga is divided into three separate components:

FIRST STAGE: postural yoga (*asana*), in which you slowly and carefully adopt particular postures, putting a muscle or group of muscles on the stretch and holding that for some seconds before unwinding. Usually you then stretch the opposite muscles, thus working around the body over the course of 20 to 60 minutes. At the end of this time, you will feel a profound sense of warmth and relaxation throughout the body, preparing you for the second stage.

SECOND STAGE: yoga meditation, which commonly uses imagery.

THIRD STAGE: breath control (*pranayama*), in which you use different parts of the lungs, as well as one nostril at a time.

Postural yoga (*asana*) can be practiced on its own.

BELOW *Yoga originates from ancient India.*

LEFT *Try to find a yoga teacher who gives classes.*

JOIN A CLASS

Although books are available that claim to be able to teach you yoga, it is probably wise to join a class at least for the early stages. You must be careful with certain medical conditions, you must not overstretch, and you will need feedback to make sure you are performing it correctly. Many people spend a lifetime learning increasingly refined forms of yoga.

WHERE AND WHEN?

Yoga can be practiced outside classes, at home, or even in the workplace, as long as you can find a few quiet moments in a warm environment. Before breakfast is an ideal time for yoga because your stomach is empty and your muscles are rested. Beginning your day with exercises will give you much-needed energy and will help you work more efficiently.

AUTOGENIC TRAINING

Autogenic training consists of learning a series
of exercises that lead to rapid and deep relaxation.

Basic autogenic training consists of six standard exercises in which you will be taught, in succession, to focus awareness of the arm feeling heavy, the hand warm, the heart calm and regular, the breathing deep, the abdomen warm, and the forehead cool. Once these techniques have been mastered, you then progress onto "intentional exercises," which are personalized phrases designed to bring about a reduction in anxiety. These may act in a similar way to hypnotic suggestion. To derive the greatest benefit, autogenic training needs to be practiced, ideally three times a day, with each session lasting about 12 minutes.

SELF DISCIPLINE

Experts who teach autogenic training recommend that exercises are practiced three times each day – each time for twelve minutes. For greatest success, this routine has to be followed without disturbance. This may be difficult if you do not have a uniform lifestyle.

GO TO A PROFESSIONAL

This method should be learned from a professional trainer, preferably someone who is skilled at dealing with the emotion that sometimes comes to the surface as you begin regular practice. It is usually taught in groups, which often helps the individual by providing support and encouragement from the experience of others. Research strongly suggests that autogenic training is genuinely helpful for treating anxiety and the associated symptoms. Autogenic training could be useful if you like to have a set pattern to follow when you relax.

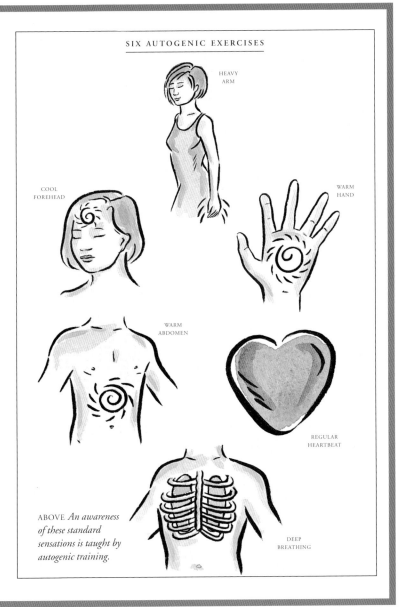

SIX AUTOGENIC EXERCISES

HEAVY
ARM

COOL
FOREHEAD

WARM
HAND

WARM
ABDOMEN

REGULAR
HEARTBEAT

DEEP
BREATHING

ABOVE *An awareness
of these standard
sensations is taught by
autogenic training.*

HYPNOSIS

Hypnosis is a method of producing a trance, which
is a state of profound relaxation of muscles and mind.

ABOVE *Try
focusing on a
clock face.*

A hypnotic trance is induced by diverting the mind away onto a monotonous sound or movement, or onto an image. Self-hypnosis can be used for relaxation, either by following an exercise such as the one opposite, or a tape recording. Hypnosis can also be performed by a therapist who will treat you by implanting suggestions in your mind, such as the idea that you no longer enjoy cigarettes, or that you are more relaxed and confident. It has been shown to be successful in suitable cases. Skilled therapists can help you deepen your trance to encourage you to uncover some aspects of your subconscious, perhaps emotions that underlie current difficulties.

SAFETY ASPECT

You need to be sure you can trust any hypnotist you see for therapy: hypnosis is the one complementary therapy that shows considerable dissatisfaction among its users. Self-hypnosis is safe if you are using it for relaxation alone, and provided you have no underlying mental disorder.

IMAGERY

People differ in the ease with which they can imagine situations. Choose scenes that are warm, with pleasant sights, sounds, and smells. The following is a general example. Take no more than 20 minutes.

ABOVE *Shamans
practiced self-
hypnosis.*

EXERCISE: SELF-HYPNOSIS WITH IMAGERY

Lie down, or sit in a relaxing arm-chair in a comfortable position. Perform a yoga deep breath exercise and let your body relax from head to toe. Imagine a beautiful country scene in the sunshine, feel the warmth, listen to the sounds, smell the flowers. Walk along the path in front of you, gently sloping down. There is a wall with a door in it: when you are ready, go through the door to the garden beyond. This is even warmer and more completely filled with flowers

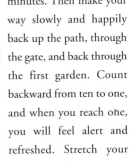

ABOVE *Imagine the smell of fresh flowers.*

with a wonderful scent. Can you see the stream farther along? Enjoy the warm, relaxing scene for a few minutes. Then make your way slowly and happily back up the path, through the gate, and back through the first garden. Count backward from ten to one, and when you reach one, you will feel alert and refreshed. Stretch your arms and legs, gently open your eyes, and look around you. Enjoy the relaxed feeling, and know that you are ready for the world, feeling more calm and deliberate than you did before.

BELOW *Imagine a beautiful landscape, stretching ahead.*

MEDITATION

Meditation, in which you focus your concentration on a single object, calms your mind and increases your awareness.

Originally, meditation was an integral part of the world's great religions, such as Buddhism and Islam, and it was used to aid spiritual progress. Meditation can produce a number of measurable changes in the body, including slower pulse, reduced blood pressure, measured breathing, increased circulation in the limbs, and more alpha rhythms in the brain waves, known to be associated with relaxation. Now that meditation's health benefits have been more widely recognized, it is often practiced without any specifically religious content.

> ## CAUTION
>
> *Do not meditate if you have had any psychiatric problems.*
>
> *Do not meditate soon after a meal or exercise.*

MIND IN NEUTRAL

The process of meditation involves reciting a single word or phrase, called a mantra, or imagining a simple image, or concentrating on your breathing, or an insoluble problem (like "the sound of one hand clapping"). The mind should be operating in neutral without any conscious control. Sometimes during a meditation, an experience known as transcendence can occur in which the person feels themselves to be outside time and space and detached from the body (in a safe, pleasant way). Transcendence is by no means necessary for the benefits of meditation; the essence of meditation is effortless concentration.

LEFT *Meditation is a Buddhist practice.*

EXERCISE: SIMPLE MEDITATION

Find a place that is quiet and where you know that you will not be disturbed. Sit erect in a comfortable chair with the head upright, hands resting palms up, feet flat on the ground. Close your eyes and relax.

● *Gently introduce the word or image you have chosen: you could use the sound "so," but do not speak it, just imagine the word attached to your breath when you breathe in. Add the word "hum" when you breathe out.*

● *Thoughts from outside will intrude; let them, and then let them go and gently steer back to your chosen word. The key is "let go" rather than trying too hard.*

● *Gently repeat the process for 20 minutes (time it).*

● *Then take a deep breath, stretch your limbs, open your eyes, and gradually return to normal.*

BELOW *Meditate somewhere quiet where you won't be disturbed.*

CLOSED EYES

HANDS PALM UPWARD

OIL BURNER

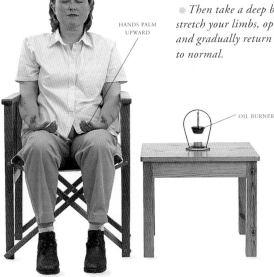

DISTURBANCE

If you are disturbed during a meditation, it is best to restart the meditation even if only for a short period, and then arouse yourself gradually, as above; rapid arousal may reduce the value of the meditation.

PHYSICAL EXERCISE

Exercise improves your mood: whether you are depressed or stressed, exercise can restore your balance.

There is now some evidence that exercise helps stress: muscle contractions stimulate particular nerve endings that send signals straight to the brain stem and hypothalamus where they release endorphins. These endorphins tend to make us calm and relaxed (they also improve the quality of sleep). They counteract the excess of cortisol in the blood, which may be caused by stress.

WHAT TYPE OF EXERCISE?

Choose a form of exercise that you are likely to carry on with. This means it must be attractive to you and you must be committed to it in some way, such as doing it with other people in a club, or getting a dog. It should be aerobic –

which means it makes you breathless: a little breathless is enough, though, and there is no need to get so breathless that you cannot talk at the same time. Anerobic exercise such as weight-lifting carries much less benefit, although you may like to see your muscles bulge!

The aim is to take moderate exercise on at least three, and preferably five, days each week. You can also do yourself a great deal of good by building exercise into your life: park the car around the corner and walk, or ignore the elevator and walk up the stairs.

LEFT *Jogging may suit some people.*

THE BENEFITS

Exercise both reduces stress and helps you to think clearly. Research shows it also improves your physical health, helping to prevent raised blood pressure, heart disease, strokes, and osteoporosis (thinning of the bones). The best news is that even a modest increase in exercise can bring great benefits in health.

ABOVE *Mountain biking is a sport that has become popular and provides exercise.*

BELOW *Swimming provides ideal exercise for those wanting all-round fitness.*

SAFETY POINTS

✧ Do not start a program of vigorous exercise if you are not already in good physical condition. You may need to consult your doctor for advice and gradually build up the level of exercise.

✧ Exercise safely: main roads are dangerous, for example. Wear appropriate clothing including safety apparatus if necessary (helmets for cyclists), and protect yourself from excessive cold in the winter.

TAI CHI

This is an ancient Chinese form of gentle relaxing exercise. It consists of 40 basic exercises and is usually taught and practiced in groups.

MASSAGE

There are some therapies involving touch that have a
pleasant, relaxing effect. The healing effect can be powerful
when we are touched in a safe therapeutic setting.

Massage was a part of medicine from the earliest records up to about the 1930s, when it was displaced by the movement toward drugs and surgery. Massage involves applying pressure with the hands moving smoothly over the body: either long, smooth strokes with the fingers, palms, or heel of the hand along the muscles; firm pressure across the fibers of the muscles; or light rhythmic stroking of the skin and superficial tissues. It can break down the tight knots that have developed over the years and relax tense muscles.

LEFT *Aromatherapy oils can be added to a base massage oil.*

AROMATHERAPY

Essential oils can have a pleasant, relaxing effect. Oils can be used in the bath, or in a vaporizer, or diluted in vegetable oil for massage. You can use oils recommended for anxiety, such as camomile, lavender, and ylang-ylang. Aromatherapists select particular oils according to the individual's personality and symptoms. The oils may have effects through the bloodstream, or they may work directly on the emotions through their effect on the nose – think of the different way you react to the scent of a rose compared with the smell of a farmyard!

CAUTION

A word of warning: some oils are strong, so you should observe the precautions on the bottle.

THE LEFT FOOT

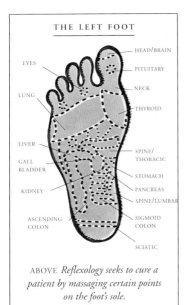

EYES
HEAD/BRAIN
PITUITARY
NECK
LUNG
THYROID
LIVER
SPINE/
THORACIC
GALL
BLADDER
STOMACH
PANCREAS
KIDNEY
SPINE/LUMBAR
ASCENDING
COLON
SIGMOID
COLON
SCIATIC

ABOVE *Reflexology seeks to cure a patient by massaging certain points on the foot's sole.*

REFLEXOLOGY

Reflexology consists of deep massage of tender points in the feet, with the aim of stimulating reflexes that affect other parts of the body. Each foot is examined in turn, looking for areas of tenderness, or the impression of crystals, which are dispersed by deep massaging motions. You are likely to feel

RIGHT *Visit a professional masseur to ease back tension.*

tired afterward, to sleep deeply, and to have dreams. It is possible that the massage releases the hormone oxytocin from the brain, which has a known relaxing effect.

SELF-HEALTH MASSAGE

Aromatherapy oils are very suitable for a relaxing self-massage, or massage from a partner, friend, or therapist. Enjoy discovering the most pleasant techniques and most productive areas, concentrating on the most stressed areas, particularly the shoulders, neck, and arms. Alternatively, you can use books to advise you where and how to use massage.

ACUPUNCTURE AND ACUPRESSURE

There are several therapies that are based on the idea
that energy flows around the body, is disturbed
in conditions such as stress, and can be corrected
by physical treatment to the system.

ACUPUNCTURE

In acupuncture, several fine needles are inserted into various points of the body and left, usually for up to 20 minutes. They produce a feeling of warmth or dull ache, or a stronger sensation called De Qi (pronounced "der chee"). Surprisingly, you hardly notice the needles as they go in – but they are needles all the same, and if you cannot bear the thought of them, don't let anyone persuade you! Depending on your belief system, the needles either correct the flow of energy or stimulate nerve endings. There is anecdotal evidence of people finding that acupuncture helps their stress, but so far little rigorous research.

ACUPRESSURE AND SHIATSU

These therapies use finger pressure on acupuncture points. Shiatsu is a Japanese therapy and adds gentle manipulation, stretching, and local massage called "anma." Pressure on the points is believed to restore normal flow in meridians. You will usually be treated fully clothed lying on the floor, while the therapist uses his or her fingers to search for, and then rub, points with the hand, elbow, or foot.

BELOW *The acupucturist
chooses points on the body
according to diagnosis.*

MERIDIANS

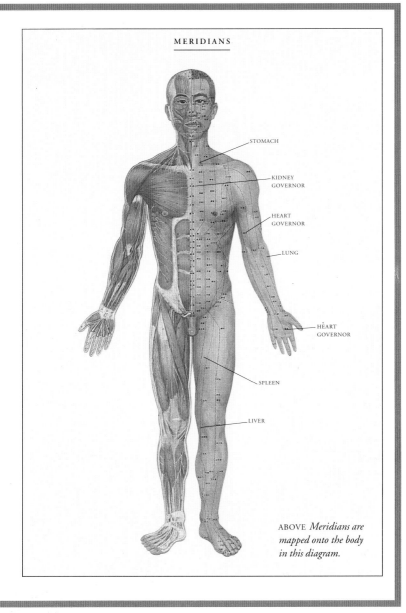

STOMACH

KIDNEY
GOVERNOR

HEART
GOVERNOR

LUNG

HEART
GOVERNOR

SPLEEN

LIVER

ABOVE *Meridians are
mapped onto the body
in this diagram.*

THE ALEXANDER TECHNIQUE

This technique is based on the idea that correct posture and body movement will release mental and physical tension.

Alexander was an Australian actor who lost his most precious asset – his voice. His physicians could find no explanation, but he discovered that the stress of appearing in public made him jut his head forward, tensing up his neck muscles, and constricting his larynx, thus reducing his voice to a squeak. He worked out that he must let his head rise up and forward, let the spine follow, and feel the body lengthen and broaden.

It is very difficult to learn the Alexander Technique from books: you really need a course of exercises with a qualified teacher to correct the bad posture. Many people find the effect rather surprising: they regain physical posture and psychological "poise," which leads to an improvement in relaxation and self-esteem.

F.M. ALEXANDER

After making his initial discovery, Alexander made further experiments and began to write about his findings in articles and books. In 1904 he came to England and started a medical practice, giving voice training to actors like Sir Henry Irving.

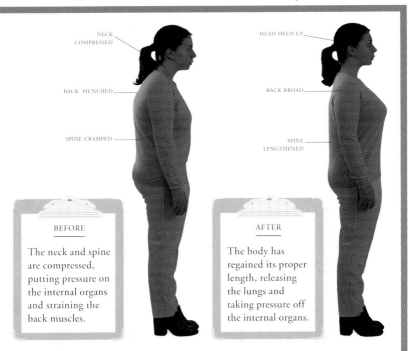

NECK
COMPRESSED

BACK HUNCHED

SPINE CRAMPED

HEAD HELD UP

BACK BROAD

SPINE
LENGTHENED

BEFORE

The neck and spine
are compressed,
putting pressure on
the internal organs
and straining the
back muscles.

AFTER

The body has
regained its proper
length, releasing
the lungs and
taking pressure off
the internal organs.

HOW ALEXANDER TECHNIQUE HELPS STRESS

LEFT *Actors use
this technique.*

Alexander technique probably helps
stress by relaxing the neck muscles
and improving the circulation of
blood and lymph. Importantly, it
will improve both the appearance
and the feel of the "sagging
abdomen," which started when you
learnt to breath properly, into your
abdomen. Many professional
musicians, actors and sportsmen use
the Alexander Technique and find it
improves their mental concentration
and physical performance.

NATURAL MEDICINES

You may feel tempted to ask the pharmacist or health-food store for a natural product, available without prescription. There are several preparations that are recommended for anxiety and insomnia. They fall into different categories.

HERBAL REMEDIES

These are derived from plants and therefore contain real chemicals, just like ordinary drugs. Some herbal remedies have calming or sedative properties, such as passiflora, skullcap, wild lettuce, and valerian, taken in tablet form. Camomile and clover blossom can be made into tea or

BELOW *Plants and flowers have been used to cure illnesses for centuries.*

infusions. Very little is known about their precise actions on the brain, or whether they are really any more useful than tranquilizers.

St. John's wort (*Hypericum*) is becoming recognized as having definite action in cases of depression. It may also prove to be useful for panic attacks. Again, nobody is sure yet how St. John's wort works, although there is some suggestion that it increases the action of serotonin in the brain rather like antidepressant drugs (see page 89).

DANDELION

THYME

ST. JOHN'S WORT

VITAMINS AND MINERALS

These are widely promoted for all sorts of conditions including stress, although there is little evidence that they are necessary except when the diet is deficient.

If you eat a varied diet with five portions of fruit or vegetables a day, you are getting virtually everything you need. If you believe your diet may be deficient then a multivitamin preparation containing vitamins B, C, E, and folic acid will meet your needs. The tablets may contain low doses of the minerals calcium, selenium, and zinc, which are probably of benefit.

ABOVE *A healthy diet provides plenty of vitamins and minerals.*

BELOW *Vitamins and mineral supplements can give the body extra energy in the battle against stress.*

WARNING

It is tempting to think that because herbs are natural, they are absolutely safe. The truth is that their safety has never been studied properly, and we just don't know. So, never exceed the stated dose, do not use for more than three days in a row, and store them well out of children's reach. If any unexpected symptoms occur, discuss your herbal remedies with your physician.

HOMEOPATHY

Homeopathic remedies are often confused with herbal remedies. Herbal remedies use concentrations of plants, while homepathic remedies use plants, minerals, and some animal products as a basis for medicine.

Homeopathy started from observing the side-effects produced in healthy volunteers who were taking fairly large

ABOVE *Homeopathic medicine often comes in the form of small white pills.*

doses of natural products – herbs, minerals, salts, and so on. Each product tended to produce a typical symptom picture.

The first principle of homeopathy is to match the symptom picture of the natural product to your symptoms as closely as possible: "Like cures like." The second principle is that the strength of the remedy is increased by

---

BACH FLOWER REMEDIES

ORNITHOGALUM
UMBELLATUM

An British physician, Dr. Edward Bach, believed that flowers had considerable healing powers. He suggested that they should only be picked at daybreak in perfect weather conditions.

The essence of the flowers is distilled off and bottled, to be taken by mouth as required. One well-known Bach flower remedy, made from a particular combination of flowers, is known as Rescue Remedy and is believed to help in any emergency situation like stress. Many people find these remedies helpful, and there are no side-effects.

diluting it. The majority of homeopathic remedies have been prepared by diluting them in 100 times their volume of water, repeated about six times. They have very little if any of the original substance left in them. Homeopaths believe that the essence of the material is still present in some way which has yet to be discovered.

RIGHT *No remedies are tested on animals, and they are available in health-food stores.*

TREATMENT

If you want to use homeopathy, you can treat yourself, choosing a remedy from the suggestions in books on the subject or leaflets at the health-food store. However, homeopathy has become extremely complicated in the 200 years or so since it was developed, so you might be better off visiting a homeopath, who will prescribe only after taking a very detailed history of your case. Perhaps the history-taking is beneficial in itself, helping you to see things in perspective.

IMPATIENS GLANDULIFERA

CLEMATIS

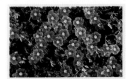

ABOVE AND LEFT *Flowers, in all their variety, are believed to have healing powers.*

HELANTHEMUM NUMMULARIUM

PRUNUS "AMANOGAWA"

DEALING WITH STRESS FACTORS

Now you are building up your resistance to stress, you are strong enough to look at the circumstances that precipitate the stress. There is only room here for a sketch since there are as many different stressful circumstances as there are stressed people.

DEALING WITH STRESS

There are at least three funda-mental approaches to dealing with stress:

1 In an ideal world, you would get rid of the stress factors in your life. Some factors can be modified, but realistically, there are many problems we are stuck with: our work and our family are ours, and that's all there is to it. What then?

2 You can change the way you respond to the stress. It is possible to change your habits. You could learn to tolerate the stress factor, to distract yourself so that it doesn't seem so important, or to mentally prepare yourself. With cognitive therapy (see later), you can identify the thought processes that lead you to experience stress and find out how you can change them.

3 You could simply run away. But that's not why you're reading this book. If you are realistic, you will recognize that running away may mean giving in which in turn could worsen feelings of stress. Changing job or lifestyle radically needs serious consideration, and this is a decision that you should put off until you have first dealt with the stress.

It is a well-known fact that certain major events in life are particularly likely to cause stress, though stress is not inevitable. These include: losing a job, changing a job, moving, having children under school age, separation or divorce, significant illness of a family member or close friend, bereavement, or retirement.

RIGHT *Major events in our lives, such as divorce, parenting, and buying a home, can be stressful.*

PROBLEMS IN YOUR PARTNERSHIP

Many stresses begin and finish here. Living with another person calls for tolerance more than anything else, a tolerance that is based on respect. Everyone has a different background, unique needs, personal expectations, and individual habits. You have chosen to be partners and have the huge privilege of intimacy together, which carries with it the responsibility of respecting each other's rights and working out solutions to your problems. You should not hesitate to ask for professional help with this most important aspect of your life.

STRESS IN THE HOME

Every role in a family brings its own peculiar pressures. Understanding your family's difficulties will benefit you and them.

MOTHERHOOD

Although motherhood can feel very satisfying and productive, it can sometimes be very frustrating. Babies do cry unaccountably, and they do wake at night. Some mothers feel themselves to be trapped in a mindless and unstimulating, yet fully responsible, position for 24 hours a day, 365 days a year. Laborious household chores may be a stark contrast to previous stimulating employment; yet a mother may feel guilty if she wants to make a life of her own.

RIGHT *Toddlers can both be a joy and a strain on your energy resources.*

CHILDREN

In addition to being wonders of innocence and endless fun, toddlers can also be impossibly demanding and disobedient, pushing their parents' patience to the very limit. Older children may be moody and keen to prove their independence. Sometimes the only way they can express themselves is by shocking their parents, perhaps by smoking, drinking, or taking drugs. Disagreement between partners on managing their children is often compounded by a lack of clear, standardized advice.

LEFT *Motherhood is one of life's most special experiences, but it is not always easy.*

FATHERHOOD

Fathers soon discover that their partner's love is now shared with a baby, often to the father's disadvantage. This can lead to both emotional and sexual frustration. There may be less money coming in but more expenses. The father's role in child-rearing can be difficult to define, and often he gets home from work to find his children worn out, miserable, and far from their best. Small children often disturb the peace at night, and restrict the possibilities for vacations, reducing the chance for much-needed rest. Frustration, particularly if linked to drinking alcohol, can all too often lead to violent outbursts.

ELDERLY RELATIVES

Couples may wish to fulfill their responsibilities to their parents by taking them into their own homes when they become less capable of independent existence. However well intentioned this idea may be, adequate space in the home is needed to live parallel lives, and both parties must have a tolerant attitude.

Some individuals accumulate bitterness and resentment throughout their life and are difficult even for saints to live with. Other elderly people have difficulty relinquishing their parental role and accepting a degree of dependency. Physical disablement and loss of faculties, particularly deafness, may be stressful both to the sufferer and to the carer. Nights may be disturbed and time off difficult.

BELOW *Physical disability can be distressing for sufferer and carer.*

STRESS AND WORK

There are, of course, countless ways in which work can be stressful. Some common examples follow, with the aim of encouraging you to think around them and recognize the acute pressures that you may be under.

ABOVE *Many people experience extreme levels of stress at work.*

Write down a list of your pressures, think about them, talk them over with an understanding friend or a professional advisor: then work out whether you can change them, or whether you must change the way they affect you.

Stresses at work can be divided into groups according to their source.

THE ORGANIZATION

Pressures typically arise from job insecurity, lack of staff, safety at work, apparently pointless regulations and restrictions, inadequate personal space, inadequate reward for initiative and effort, poor channels of communication. Feelings of lack of control over your work, with inability to influence and change the system, are known to be particularly stressful. But it is worth remembering that the organization itself can provide structure and security in life, and these are important in combating stress.

MANAGEMENT ISSUES

Bullying or lack of empathy from managers, absence of credit for good performance, inadequate role definition, bad decisions on promotion (in other words, others are promoted ahead of you!) are classic examples. But remember, no boss is all bad, and the next one may be much worse.

COLLEAGUES

Harassment (whether physical or sexual), inefficiency, interpersonal problems, complainers and loud-mouths, competition (for example, for status) can all cause stress. But remember, colleagues can show an enormous degree of empathy, support, and advice at times of stress, which can provide great relief.

PHYSICAL CONDITIONS

Shift work, poor ergonomics, especially the arrangement of computer stations, excessive noise, physically repetitive work, poor air quality, lack of outside view (important for some), and failure to take a proper lunch break are all potent causes of stress.
One of the most common of all stresses is having too much to do and too little time to do it. Learning time-management skills can be very valuable at helping you organize both your space and time so you establish your priorities, learn to delegate, and avoid duplication of effort.

ABOVE *Your working environment is a crucial factor in stress control.*

STRESS AND
THE ENVIRONMENT

Ideally, your environment should offer you tranquility and
relaxation to combat the stress elsewhere in your life.

POTENTIAL SOURCES OF STRESS

Here are some features of many people's existence that they might regard as crucial: stress may arise when they are threatened:

A SAFE HOME

No unwanted changes or neighborhood development

Confidence in pillars of society at local, state, and national level

Adequate living space

Surrounded by pleasing and attractive objects

Sunshine and blue skies - if only!

Control over noise levels

Equable and non-interfering neighbors

Freedom from local crime and delinquency

National economic prosperity

GOOD GOVERNMENT

International security and prosperity

PROSPERITY

Confidence in government

SECURITY

THE MEDIA

We are deluged with news, much of it bad and producing stress in various ways. For example, reports of starvation in the deserts may move us, but it can also make us feel helpless, even guilty for eating. We should recognize that we cannot do everything in this world: if we help our neighbor, that is a good start. A second common source of worry is health scares, especially over food,

which we feel is so important. It may be worth becoming a little more cynical about why people publish bad news: the researchers need the publicity, and the media need the stories. The anxiety generated by these scares is frequently out of all proportion to the degree of genuine risk. Sometimes it's better not to watch the news!

LEFT *In modern society we are constantly made aware of potential disaster.*

POST-TRAUMATIC STRESS DISORDER

This is when victims of a sudden, overwhelming catastrophic event suffer an intensified stress reaction. Some victims may respond with immediate numbness or panic, followed by a particular form of anxiety. They may re-experience the drama in daydreams or in nightmares; they may avoid getting involved with other people and other events for fear of experiencing fresh emotions; and they may suffer marked sleep disturbance and irritability together with an exaggerated startle response.

It has become standard practice to offer counseling immediately after the traumatic event, and help from skilled professionals is a good way to treat post-traumatic stress disorder.

RIGHT *Post-traumatic stress disorder can silence and numb sufferers.*

PSYCHOTHERAPY

Psychotherapy means treatment by talking rather than by drugs. There are times when help from outside can be valuable, even though in the last resort it is you who is the expert in your own stress, and you who are therefore best at managing it. There are different types of therapy on offer.

PSYCHIATRIST

This is a physician who has undergone specialist training in psychiatry, for at least three academic years. Psychiatrists usually work in a clinic or hospital, or they belong to a private practice, either working alone or with other professionals. They deal with a whole range of mental illnesses. Many psychiatrists have developed special skills and interests: some are more familiar with drugs, others prefer to use psychotherapy, and many combine the best of both.

ABOVE *The psychologist compiles notes about his or her patient.*

PSYCHOLOGIST

Anyone who studies psychology in a recognized degree course may be known as a psychologist. He or she usually has an M.A. or a Ph.D., and can receive additional training to become a clinical psychologist.

PSYCHOTHERAPISTS

Psychotherapy is usually practiced by a psychiatrist or a psychologist, either by itself or combined with various medical treatments.

IS IT EFFECTIVE?

Despite sometimes being called "superficial," psychotherapy can be very helpful at preventing anxiety from getting hold, particularly in the early stages. It involves listening to the problems, providing explanations for the symptoms, accepting you – which is important for your self-esteem – reassuring you that stress is common and comes and goes, and offering straightforward advice on helpful measures and attitudes. With luck, you have some valuable friend who can do this quite naturally, and many doctors have developed skills in superficial psychotherapy.

BELOW *The psychotherapist may encourage a patient to remember the past.*

COUNSELING

This is a more detailed form of therapy that goes further than superficial psychotherapy. There are very many different individual approaches, and much of the benefit may depend on the relationship that develops. You will be able to recognize counselors who will be helpful to you if they respond to you with empathy, respect, and warmth. Counselors should have recognized qualifications.

BELOW *Childhood experiences are formative and may have to be explored during counseling.*

WILL IT WORK?

✧ The counselor will have empathy, i.e. you feel they are in tune with your experiences.

✧ You will feel that you are being accepted for your own personal worth.

✧ The relationship between you and the counselor will feel harmonious and safe.

If you do not get these feelings, then you may need to change your counselor.

BEHAVIOR THERAPY

This approach looks at your response to stressful events, the reaction you have learned or developed subconsciously. Behavioral therapists – unlike psychiatrist, psychologists, and counselors – do not look for underlying causes, but teach you to isolate and then recognize stressful events. They then look at ways to relieve your condition by suggesting and applying relaxation techniques to suit you. It's as if learning how to behave in a relaxed way makes you feel more relaxed. Behavior therapy may also be useful for people who suffer from phobias, who can be helped to face up to the phobic situation while staying calm and relaxed, a process called desensitization.

COGNITIVE THERAPY

The basis of cognitive therapy works on the assumption that your way of thinking about the stress factor has become distorted, for whatever reasons. Cognitive therapists encourage you to sit down and think about the causes of your stress objectively, you may recognize that your reaction to a challenge has not been logical or even appropriate.

During this type of treatment, the therapist needs to be sensitive in helping you to realize this, because you cannot at first believe that there is another way to respond. Cognitive therapy helps you identify distorted thoughts, then establish more logical thoughts and apply them in real life.

ABOVE *A cognitive therapist may encourage you to write a rational list of your problems.*

Cognitive and behavior therapies have been shown to have good short-term and long-term results in treating stress, and may be combined for a greater impact.

GROUP THERAPY

You may be offered therapy in a group. This has certain advantages - you can see that other people have similar problems, they can help you with fresh insights into your own problems, and they can be honest about spotting when you are not making an effort or are subconsciously blocking your progress. Group leaders need special training and skills.

PSYCHOANALYSIS

This is quite a different approach that aims to get at the underlying reasons why you are responding in this way to the stress factors, whether it is something in your personality you need to change, or something in your background that you need to come to terms with. This involves a considerable commitment of time, effort, and money. There are several different styles of psychoanalysis, named after their inventors (Freudian, Jungian). Some people find such therapy very successful in helping them "find their real self."

BELOW *You may wish to visit a therapist with the rest of your family.*

SIGMUND FREUD

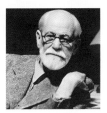

Sigmund Freud was born in 1856 and studied medicine before specializing in neurology. His seminal work *The Interpretation of Dreams* outlined his major theories of psycholanalysis.

LIFE-SKILLS TRAINING PROGRAMS

We usually learn skills in relating with other people as we grow older, but sometimes this just doesn't happen. The skill most commonly missing is assertiveness (which is not at all the same as aggressiveness!). Assertiveness training helps you to identify your own purpose and express it clearly in a way that is acceptable to other people. Ideally, they come to agree with you: if not, you can negotiate to achieve your ends without hurting them needlessly.

DRUG TREATMENTS

You have probably chosen this book
in order to avoid drugs. Many physicians,
too, are becoming more reluctant to prescribe
drugs for stress, except in special cases,
which we will mention.

The worry about drugs started with the benzodiazepines, which first seemed to solve the whole problem of stress, but then were discovered to be far from perfect.

BENZODIAZEPINES

The human brain has its own benzodiazepines, similar to the drug form (diazepam). What they do is to detach the reacting part of the brain from its other activities. So anything can happen, and you don't mind because you are tranquilized.

The advantage of benzodiazepines is that they blunt your response to serious problems, and they are very useful for a week or two during a crisis. The problems with them are that they interfere with your memory, make you drowsy, become less effective so you need higher doses, and interact with alcohol, which can be dangerous. They also react strongly on people with breathing disorders, and they reduce your ability to learn new skills. In short, they don't treat stress; they merely stop you from feeling it.

DEPENDENCY

It is now clear that benzodiazepines may cause dependency in a small proportion of those who take them, which means they feel withdrawal symptoms when they stop taking them. This is worse than just

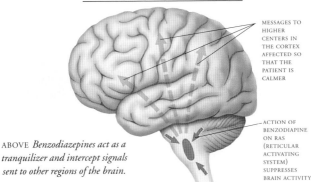

EFFECTS OF BENZODIAZEPINES

MESSAGES TO HIGHER CENTERS IN THE CORTEX AFFECTED SO THAT THE PATIENT IS CALMER

ACTION OF BENZODIAPINE ON RAS (RETICULAR ACTIVATING SYSTEM) SUPPRESSES BRAIN ACTIVITY

ABOVE *Benzodiazepines act as a tranquilizer and intercept signals sent to other regions of the brain.*

LEFT *Always follow your physician's instructions when taking drugs.*

the recurrence of the anxiety: people become very agitated and jumpy, suffer disturbed and disturbing thoughts, and insomnia that may go on for a few weeks. The only way to avoid these withdrawal symptoms is to tail the dose of drugs off very slowly, over many weeks, which requires a sustained effort of self-control that many people find difficult.

SUMMARY

Benzodiazepines can be very comforting to people for specific trauma, but are currently not used for long-term medication. It seems there never will be a Magic Bullet for stress, and that it is part of life's inevitable training that we shall all have to learn to handle our own stress.

BUSPIRONE

This is a new type of tranquilizer that seems to have much less risk of dependency than the benzodiazepines, although there have been early reports of mild withdrawal symptoms, and the drug takes longer to affect anxiety symptoms than benzodiazepines.

BETA-BLOCKERS

These drugs may help to suppress some of the uncomfortable physical symptoms of stress, although they don't help remove the source of the underlying fear and agitation, and should perhaps be used in the short-term to alleviate rather than cure stess.

They work by blocking the action of the sympathetic nervous system on the heart (see page 13), so they can reduce the fast heart-rate and palpitations that worsen panic. Since these symptoms can feed back into the brain and increase the stress, beta-blockers may be useful in the short term to make you feel more comfortable. They are especially valuable to anyone who already suffers from heart problems.

HOW BETA-BLOCKERS WORK

SIGNALS (NERVE IMPULSES FROM BRAIN)

SYMPATHETIC NERVE PATH

BETA BLOCKERS IN HEART MUSCLE STOP SIGNALS SENT THROUGH SYMPATHETIC NERVOUS SYSTEM FROM REACHING BETA RECEPTORS

ABOVE *Beta-blockers repel signals from the brain that cause palpitations.*

ANTIDEPRESSANTS

ABOVE *Depression affects one in five people directly; it also affects other family members.*

There are two situations in stress where antidepressants can be useful. They may help if you were depressed before you became anxious, or if you have panic attacks that caused the stress in the first place. In suitable cases, antidepressants may actually treat the fundamental problem and not just the symptoms. Increasingly, psychiatrists are looking with interest to see whether antidepressants might even help people with stress alone: some find them helpful, although the agitation may be increased for a week or two, which may cause problems.

The most modern antidepressants have fewer side-effects than the "traditional" drugs first prescribed for depression, but do not appear to be more effective, despite being very much more expensive. Fortunately, antidepressants do not produce dependency or withdrawal symptoms.

RIGHT
Antidepressants can be prescribed by your physician and may help stress.

REMEMBER

There is a strong tendency for stress to become a much diminished problem as we proceed through our lives: the difficulties, challenges, and battles are associated with the second and third decades of life for most people. Later, there may be more time to relax, for example when children have left home, and greater maturity, which often brings tolerance and greater skills in looking after ourselves and meeting our  own needs. Don't make a habit of stress; beat it right now, starting with a positive approach and the methods and techniques in this book.

FURTHER READING

Fontana, D.
Managing Stress
(British Psychological Society)

Hartley, M.
The Good Stress Guide
(Sheldon Press)

Patel, C.
The Complete Guide to Stress Management
(Optima)

Pietroni, P.
The Guide to Alternative Healthcare
(Simon & Schuster)

Weekes, C.
Peace from Nervous Suffering
(Angus and Robertson)

Weekes, C.
Self-Help for your Nerves
(Angus and Robertson)

INDEX

ALSO IN THIS SERIES

Picture Acknowledgments

a=above; b=below; r=right